FRONT LINE JAZZ
PIANO SOLOS

Transcribed by
BRIAN PRIESTLEY

FROM THE ORIGINAL RECORDINGS
AND PERFORMANCES OF:

DUKE ELLINGTON
OSCAR PETERSON
HORACE SILVER
BUD POWELL
HERBIE HANCOCK
ERROL GARNER
FATS WALLER
CHICK COREA
EARL HINES
AHMAD JAMAL

BRIAN PRIESTLEY is the presenter of a weekly jazz
programme on BBC Radio London, and the author of the
recently published biography of composer Charles Mingus. He
is also, when time permits, a pianist who has appeared at such
clubs as Ronnie Scott's and the Pizza Express, and teaches a
jazz piano course at Goldsmiths' College in south-east London.
Several of the transcriptions were originally commissioned by
the College, and are reproduced here with permission.

First Published 1983
© International Music Publications

Exclusive Distributors
International Music Publications
60/70 Roden Street, Ilford, England

1-2-50909

FOREWORD

It is perhaps reassuring that even the great pianists play wrong notes occasionally. Since these solos are transcribed from actual recordings, wrong notes played cleanly are retained while misfingered notes are represented by 'x'. Notes played very lightly ('ghosted') are shown in brackets.

The tempo markings are in each case those of the recorded performances, but it is worth pointing out that with due care and attention to timing and phrasing, each solo can be made to swing successfully at as much as 40% less than the original speed.

Chord sequences have been shown in a relatively simple form, even where there is considerable deviation in the piano part. In this way, the deviations may be appreciated as such, and accompanying players such as bassists or guitarists can have a basic sequence to work from. With the exception of a couple of shorter pieces, the chord symbols are only given for the first chorus. The intention is that even the pianist should memorise the sequence, and apply its lessons not only to the subsequent transcribed choruses but also, as soon as possible, to his or her own improvisations.

DUKE ELLINGTON

DUKE ELLINGTON's version of *Body and Soul* is an excellent demonstration of his orchestral approach to keyboard textures, and you can hear the solo equally well as being conceived in terms of trumpets, saxophones and clarinets. The performance from Ellington's trio album, 'Piano in the Foreground', (CBS 84419) uses the original chords for bars 18-20 rather than the elaborated version popularised by Art Tatum.

OSCAR PETERSON

The OSCAR PETERSON improvisation on *Tea for Two* immediately followed the Lester Young solo which was transcribed in 'Front Line Sax Solos' (a recording last reissued, at the time of writing, on Verve 2683 058). The performer's ebullient right-hand style, influenced by the piano work of Nat King Cole, is well captured in these two choruses.

HORACE SILVER

The film theme *The Night Has A Thousand Eyes* — not to be confused with the 1960's pop song of the same name — has been recorded by John Coltrane, Sonny Rollins and Stan Getz among others, but the first jazz version was that of HORACE SILVER (issued on Philips and Epic but currently hard to find). The chorus structure should be 48 bars long (A-A-B) but the continuity of Silver's witty and highly rhythmic solo survives the accidental omission of 16 bars from his second chorus.

BUD POWELL

JEROME KERN's harmonic sequence for *All The Things You Are* not only changes key several times but has chords built on all twelve notes of the chromatic scale and is therefore the classic example of a logical use of the 'circle of fourths'. This particular BUD POWELL solo is part of the same performance as that of Coleman Hawkins shown in Front Line Sax Solos (Black Lion BLP 30125) and makes an interesting contrast with Powell's slower-tempo version at the famous Massey Hall concert with Dizzy Gillespie and Charlie Parker.

HERBIE HANCOCK

HERBIE HANCOCK's *All of You*, recorded as a member of the Miles Davis quintet (Miles in Europe, CBS EMB 31103), gains much of its impetus from alternating the 'dotted' 12/8 feeling of the first chorus with bursts of 16/16, all against the basic time signature of 4/4. It should be noted that from bar 65 to the end, the chord sequence is abandoned and replaced by 4-bar 'turnarounds', (e.g. Fm7 / Bb7 / Gm7 / C7) an idea popularised by Erroll Garner and Ahmad Jamal and adopted by Hancock's predecessors in the David group, namely Red Garland and Wynton Kelly.

ERROL GARNER

The ERROLL GARNER approach to the traditional theme *Frankie And Johnny* is the only 12-bar blues sequence in the book, and the influence of the blues is strongly felt in the right-hand ornamentation of the tune. In this unaccompanied performance (issued on Spotlite SPJ 129) Garner's left-hand retains the 'stride piano' style with updated chord voicings such as 9ths and flattened 13ths, but occasionally breaks out into an independent line.

FATS WALLER

Stylistically the earliest variety of jazz piano to be found in this volume, *When you and I were young, Maggie*, by FATS WALLER (sandwiched between two vocals on EMI One-Up OUM 2086) departs from the original tune considerably but uses it as a jumping-off point at the start of each 8-bar section. The left-hand, although in a striding 4/4, switches to the two-beat (2/2) feel of ragtime in bars 49-54 and shows other ways of varying the texture to avoid becoming monotonous.

CHICK COREA

Kurt Weill's A-B-A-C chorus (bars 2-33) to *This is New* here benefits from the extension of the last 2 bars to 8, in a modal section which counterbalances the constant key changes hitherto. This performance by CHICK COREA (last available on Atlantic ATL 50326) reflects the influence of McCoy Tyner, both in some of the right-hand lines and in the use of chords built in intervals of a fourth, e.g. root-4th-7th or 3rd-6th-9th.

EARL HINES

The EARL HINES improvisation on the famous *Maple Leaf Rag* (recorded with his big band on Coral CP 63) illustrates well the differences between ragtime and jazz. The left-hand part, while occasionally alluding to the straightforward accompaniment of ragtime, is much more irregular and complementary to the right-hand, which, although it briefly refers to the original tune, makes free play with new melodic ideas; unexpected accents; the contrast between single notes and octaves; arpeggios; glissando — you name it, he does it!

AHMAD JAMAL

AHMAD JAMAL's *Billy Boy* was not only a jukebox hit in its day but widely influential on other pianists (it is included in the valuable Jazz Piano Anthology, CBS 67257). Jamal deserves the credit for borrowing Erroll Garner's idea of synchronising left-hand chording with the notes of the right-hand melody in a way which can be traced in the work of every pianist since then. See for instance, above solos by Herbie Hancock and Chick Corea.

FRONT LINE JAZZ PIANO SOLOS

Transcribed by
BRIAN PRIESTLEY

BODY AND SOUL

Words by ROBERT SOUR,
EDWARD HEYMAN & FRANK EYTON
Music by JOHN GREEN

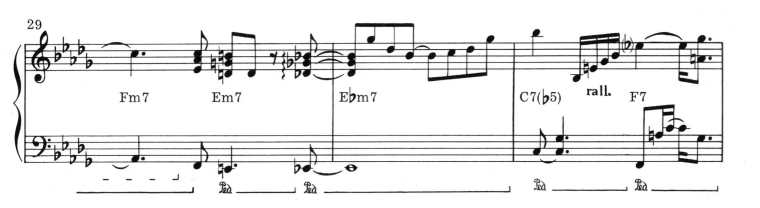

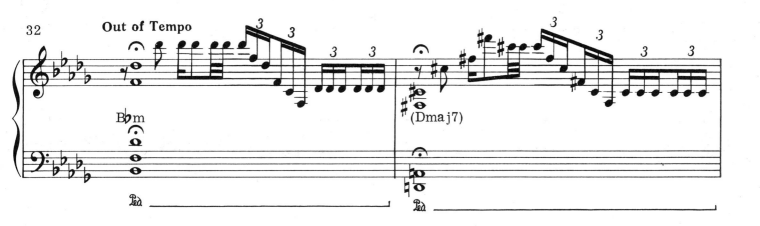

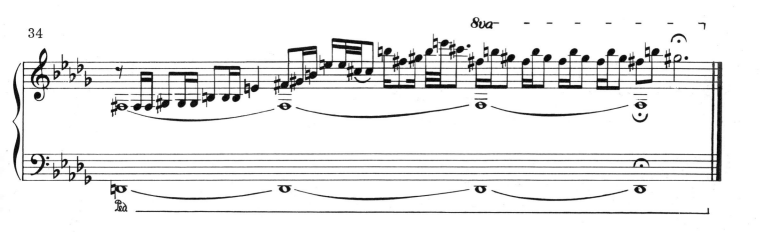

TEA FOR TWO

Words by IRVING CAESAR
Music by VINCENT YOUMANS

THE NIGHT HAS A THOUSAND EYES

Words by BUDDY BERNIER
Music by JERRY BRAININ

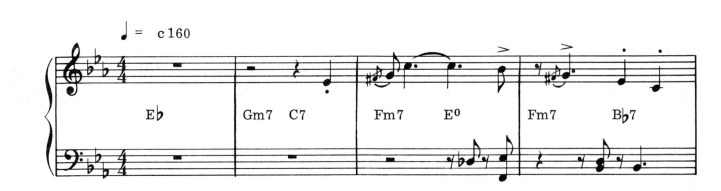

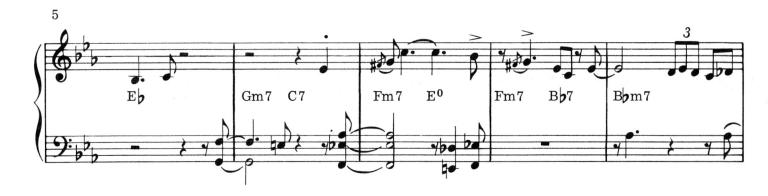

ALL THE THINGS YOU ARE

Words by OSCAR HAMMERSTEIN II
Music by JEROME KERN

ALL OF YOU

Words & Music by COLE PORTER

FRANKIE AND JOHNNY

TRADITIONAL

WHEN YOU AND I WERE YOUNG, MAGGIE

Words by GEORGE W. JOHNSON
Music by J. A. BUTTERFIELD

THIS IS NEW

Words by IRA GERSHWIN
Music by KURT WEILL

MAPLE LEAF RAG

By SCOTT JOPLIN

BILLY BOY

TRADITIONAL

Printed in England by West Central Printing Co. Ltd., London and Suffolk